NOSY
The Passover Lamb

written by Karen J. Pettingell, Ph.D.

illustrated by Debra Hoskins

Nosy The Passover Lamb

Written by Karen J. Pettingell, Ph.D.

Illustrated by Debra Hoskins

© 2017 by Frankie Dove Publishing

All rights reserved
This book may not be reproduced in whole or in part, in any form or by any means, electronic or mechanical, including photocopying, recording, or by any information storage and retrieval system now known or hereafter invented, without written permission from the publisher.

ISBN 978-0-9987731-0-0

Designed by George Pettingell
Edited by Bev Fowler
Typography: Adobe New Century Schoolbook

Published by Frankie Dove Publishing
P. O. Box 3875
Federal Way, Washington 98063

Dedication

This book is dedicated to my Dad, Ellsworth Leegard, and others like him who read to children. You create a love for reading and making special memories.

Some of my happiest memories as a child are Dad reading to us (I have one sister and two brothers). Each night we'd play the same game. Dad would ask which story we wanted him to read. We'd always request our favorite story.

Dad would say, "I think I've read that story before." We'd assure him that he hadn't. By this time we were all laughing and thoroughly enjoying the game. As Dad read, he would use different voices, make sounds, and tease us.

One story wasn't enough. Part of the game was getting Dad to read one more story which ended up being three or four stories. Dad reading to us was the perfect end to our day.

Thank you, Dad, for reading to me.

Karen

"Tee hee hee! Tee hee hee!"

"Who's that?" asked Baa Shirley Lamb.

"Look up in that tree, Baa Shirley," said Baa Linda.

"Tee hee hee! Tee hee hee!"

"No, the sound is coming from that bush over there," said Baa Shirley.

"Tee hee hee! Tee hee hee!"

"Come out!" called Baa Shirley. "Come out from wherever you're hiding! Fly over here, Franklin Bernard Dove. I recognize your weird laugh. You big tease! Come over here and meet my friend, Baa Linda."

"Hi, Baa Linda," said Frankie. "It's been a long time since I last saw you, Baa Shirley. I wanted to find out how you are."

"And you wanted to tease us," said Baa Shirley.

"I couldn't resist teasing you. I sat in that tree for more than five minutes and sang two songs just awful.

"You two were so busy talking, you didn't even notice me. You sure are serious. Are you okay, Baa Shirley? I see suffalation on your face."

"Frankie, there's no such word as *suffalation*. What do you mean, 'suffalation'?"

"Baa Shirley, when I look at your face, I see suffering and elation at the same time. Get it? *Suff-ering* and e-*lation*."

"Oh, brother, Frankie, you're just making up words! I still don't know what you mean. Why do you use such big words? What do *suffering* and *elation* mean?

"Well, Baa Shirley, suffering is a sadness that hurts so bad, it goes down to your toes.

"Elation is a big, big, big happiness that tingles way up to the top of your head. Your face is both very happy and very sad.

"It's *suffalation*. How can that be, Baa Shirley?"

"Frankie, I don't know if I can tell you my story, but I'll try…"

It all started about a year ago. It was early spring, and there were lots of new green leaves on the plants. I had a baby boy barely one year old. He was perfect, and didn't have even one spot on him! I called him Nosy, because when he wanted me to play with him, he would push his nose into my belly. Good thing I'm not ticklish! I still laugh at how funny it looked when Nosy would hide his nose in my woolly belly.

We lived in Egypt, in a town that had two parts. Our home was in the Hebrew part of town. We were slaves of the Egyptians, which meant that we had to do whatever they wanted us to do.

I don't know anything about where the Egyptians lived, because I was too afraid to go there. Besides, we had too much fun where we lived to care what the Egyptian part of town was like.

Each morning all the baby lambs got together and played. One day Nosy and I were walking to where the lambs were playing. Soon I noticed Nosy walking very, very strangely.

"One, two, three, hic-hop," he said. "One, two, three, hic-hop. One, two, three, hic-hop."

Each time Nosy said, "hic-hop," he jumped up.

Soon he was giggling so hard he could barely say, "One, two, three hic-hop."

"Nosy, what are you doing?" I asked.

"Mom, my legs and feet have the hic-ups. Hic-hops! Get it? Hic-ups, hic-hops!"

Nosy was giggling so hard, I started laughing, too.

Soon I was going, "One, two, three hic-hop!" along with Nosy.

We were both giggling.

That night as Nosy lay fast asleep beside me, he started to giggle in his sleep. His legs moved as if he were jumping. He was dreaming about his legs and feet having the hic-hops. I laughed.

Soon I was asleep and having fun dreams, too.

The next morning barking woke me up.

"Dusty, be quiet!" I said.

Benjamin, our owner, had a big hairy dog. We called him Dusty, because he had a huge bushy tail that dragged along the ground and made a big cloud of dust wherever he walked.

Benjamin was trying to teach him to be a sheep dog. We teased Dusty by not doing what he wanted.

"Get up! I need to take you to a new field," said Dusty. Slowly I got up and joined the rest of the sheep.

"Hey, Dusty, come catch me!" Baa Linda yelled. "I'm going to get a drink of water at the river!"

"Please don't leave the flock," said Dusty as he ran after her.

"Hey, Dusty! Look at me. I'm going to the Egyptians' part of town," said Mr. Wooley.

"Stay here with the flock, Mr. Wooley."

The more Dusty ran after us, the more we went in different directions. All the time Dusty's tail was dragging on the ground, and soon there was a big, big cloud of dust.

"Oh! Look at you, Baa Linda," I said, laughing very hard. "Your white wool is brown from the dust."

"Look at *you*," said Baa Linda. "You're so brown that Nosy sneezes every time he nudges your belly. You have a big muddy spot on your belly where Nosy sneezed."

We were all brown and dirty from the dust cloud. We sure did have fun getting Dusty to run after us!

"Dusty!" yelled Benjamin. "Get over here! Why are the lambs still here and not in the field?"

Dusty just looked sad.

"Look at all the dust on the lambs. They're dirty. Dusty, I'm very mad at you. Go to bed without any dinner."

Slowly, sadly, Dusty walked to a tree and lay down. He had been so busy trying to get us to go to the field that he did not eat lunch. Now he was not going to get dinner, either.

All the lambs got together and talked and laughed. The more we laughed and joked, the sadder and lonelier Dusty looked as he lay all by himself. Tears ran down his face and splashed in the dirt. Soon there was a big mud puddle under Dusty's nose.

The next day, Benjamin changed his mind, and we did not have to go to the field.

Three days later, Benjamin came and took my baby, Nosy.

"Come with me, Nosy," said Benjamin. "I've got a very special job for you."

For four days Benjamin's family took very good care of Nosy.

"Come play with me, Nosy," said Benjamin's son, Saul.

Soon Nosy was giggling in his special way as they played Hide-n-Seek. I watched them and, before I knew it, I was sleeping.

I was awakened when Saul came over to me and put his arms around my neck. He hid his face deep in my wool and cried so hard his whole body shook.

Poor Saul, I thought. *I wonder what could have happened to make him so sad.*

Finally Saul said, "Oh, Baa Shirley, Nosy is dead. He was my best friend."

Then I cried, too. The two of us cried for a long time. We both loved Nosy.

"Saul, come into the house and get ready for supper," said Benjamin.

Slowly, sadly, Saul went into the house. Then Benjamin put some of Nosy's blood on the doorposts of his house.

Each time I looked up and saw the doorposts with Nosy's blood on them, I thought of my perfect baby. Sadness filled every part of me. I just lay down and cried so hard that my whole body shook. I closed my eyes so I wouldn't have to look at Nosy's blood on the doorposts.

As I lay there crying, I felt something gentle on my cheek, wiping my face. I opened my eyes. It was Dusty. He was licking away my tears, hoping he could make my sadness go away.

That night he lay beside me to keep me warm.

Baa Shirley, do you hear that?" whispered Dusty.

"No. I don't hear anything. It is really, really quiet."

"That's what I mean. It is never this quiet. I don't even hear one dog barking. But if you listen closely, lots of dogs are howling in the Egyptian part of town."

"You're right! In the Egyptian part of town it is very, very noisy. All the dogs are howling. Even the humans are crying. What a strange night! I"m glad you are beside me, Dusty."

That was the longest and saddest night of my life.

The next day, Benjamin woke Dusty early to get us sheep moving.

Baa Linda, my best friend, had seen how kind and loving Dusty was to me.

"Let's do just as Dusty wants," said Baa Linda to all the sheep. "Dusty was Baa Shirley's friend all night even though we were mean to him. Let's make Dusty the best sheep dog ever. I don't want him to have to go to bed hungry or lonely again."

We quickly followed Dusty as he and Benjamin and all the Hebrew people left Egypt. God had told Moses—our leader—to get all of us out of Egypt very, very fast.

For days we were led by Moses. We walked and walked. Dusty made sure all Benjamin's lambs were safe. Benjamin often said that Dusty was the best sheep dog ever.

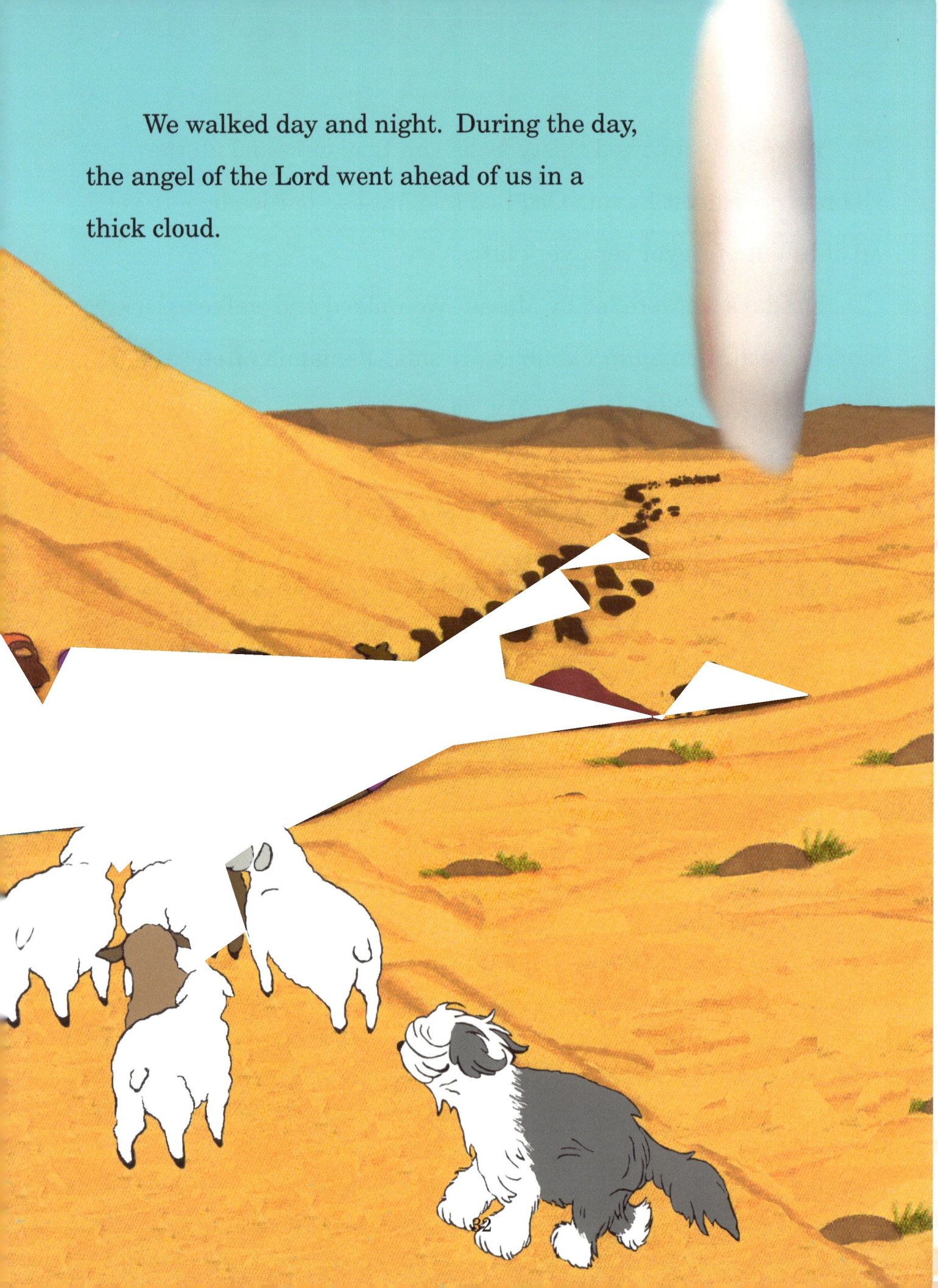

We walked day and night. During the day, the angel of the Lord went ahead of us in a thick cloud.

At night we could see where we were going, because the Lord led us as a pillar of flaming fire.

Then we stopped by a great big body of water called the Red Sea.

Suddenly we heard loud sounds.

"What's that, Daddy?" asked Saul.

"It is the Egyptians," said Benjamin. "They have come to kill us."

"Daddy, look at how many soldiers, horses, and chariots they have. What are we going to do?"

"Moses, why didn't you leave us alone in Egypt?" asked Benjamin's friend, Ira. "I would rather be a slave in Egypt than dead in this desert!"

"Yes, why didn't you leave us alone?" cried lots of other men.

Moses turned around and said, "Don't be afraid. God will save us today. Don't waver in your faith in the Lord. The Egyptians that you see now, you will never see again. This is the Lord's fight. Be quiet."

Then the angel of the Lord, who was in the cloud, moved from in front of us to behind us. We could not see the Egyptians through the cloud.

"Come, Baa Linda," I said. "Let's get close to Dusty. I'm afraid."

"I'm afraid, too," Dusty told us. "Let's pray to the Lord."

"Good idea," said Baa Linda.

We all stood still and prayed.

As we were praying, Moses walked by us. His robe gently brushed me, and I looked up. He walked over to the Red Sea and held up his walking stick.

Our quiet day was no longer quiet. A wind started to blow over the Red Sea. All day and night it blew and blew.

"Wow! Look!" I said to Baa Linda. "There's a path across the Red Sea. It's so dry that there isn't even one mud puddle."

"Come on! Hurry!" said Moses. "Quickly. Everyone must walk on the dry path to the other side of the Red Sea."

"Dusty, get the sheep moving to the other side," said Benjamin. "Hurry, before the Egyptians come."

"Dusty, I don't want to walk on the path," said Baa Linda. "All that water on both sides scares me. Look how high the water is. What if it comes rushing back?"

"Please, Baa Linda, walk with me," said Dusty. "This is what the Lord told Moses to do. We have to do what the Lord wants."

"How are you doing, Baa Shirley?" Benjamin asked me.

All I could do was look brave. My heart was very, very sad because I missed Nosy. Now I had to walk on a path with cold water on both sides. It was like walking down a long hall with the walls made of water. I didn't dare touch the water, because I didn't want it to leak and come rushing down on me. I had to trust in the Lord.

Benjamin saw the fear and pain in my eyes and tenderly picked me up.

"It's okay to cry, Baa Shirley," said Benjamin. "Nosy was Saul's best friend. They had a lot of fun. Put your head on my shoulder. I'll dry your tears."

In Benjamin's arms I felt safe. Not one of my tears fell on the dry path. He dried them all.

Quickly we went to the other side of the Red Sea. I could hear the Egyptians. All their chariots, horses, and soldiers made a sound like loud, loud thunder.

"Oh, no! The Egyptians are coming fast," said Ira to Benjamin. They're going to catch us!"

"Our Lord will defend us," said Benjamin.

The Lord did protect us.

Just then the Egyptians started acting strangely. They could not steer their chariots. The wheels of the chariots were falling off.

The Egyptians turned around to get away from the Lord. Before they could retreat off the path, the Lord told Moses to raise his hand over the Red Sea. As he did, the walls of water crumbled and flooded the dry path. All the Egyptians drowned.

The Lord had saved the Hebrew people as He promised.

"Our Lord is great!" said Benjamin and the other men. "He did not let the Egyptians keep us as slaves or kill us. We will follow the Lord's servant, Moses."

As we all stood there amazed, all the Hebrews started to sing and dance to the Lord.

> "The Lord is my strength and song, and He is become my salvation. He is my God...the Lord shall reign forever and ever..."

As we sang praises to the Lord, Benjamin held me in his arms. His deep voice soothed me as I kept my head on his shoulder.

"Remember that strange night in Egypt?" Benjamin whispered to me. I closed my eyes to try to stop the tears. It was no use. The tears escaped and ran down my cheeks.

"Our precious son, Saul, lives because of your dear Nosy's blood on the doorposts," said Benjamin. "The Lord's angel passed over our house when he saw Nosy's blood. If the angel had not gone by, Saul would have died. How can I ever tell you how much Nosy's blood means to me?"

Benjamin was quiet for a long time and held me close.

For months as we traveled, I watched Benjamin's son, Saul, closely. He was very, very cute and smiled as his parents played with him. I felt very happy to know he was alive because of Nosy, yet I felt sad because I loved and missed Nosy.

How can I be so happy and so sad at the same time? I thought.

I guess it was *suffalation*.

"Come, Baa Shirley," said Saul. "Mom gave me some special food for you and your friends, Frankie and Baa Linda. Let's play!"

He giggled as he ran to play with us.

Saul, Baa Shirley, Baa Linda, and Frankie played until Saul had to go home to have supper. They then ate the very tasty food Saul's mom had made for them.

"Come, let's sit by the tent," said Frankie.

"Frankie, we are no longer slaves," said Baa Shirley. "We are God's people! I also have another friend, Dusty. The Lord is good! I had Nosy for a whole year. Benjamin's son, Saul, lives because of Nosy, and now we are going home to the land God has promised to give us!

"Truly, the song of praise the Hebrews sang after crossing the Red Sea is true." Together the friends sang:

"The Lord is my strength and song, and He is become my salvation. He is my God...the Lord shall reign forever and ever!"

    To read about the first Passover in the Scriptures, read Exodus 12:1-8, 11-17, 21-33, 13:17-18, and 13:20-14:31.

Dear Reader,

Our dear Lord experienced SUFFALATION. He suffered so very, very much when He saw His Son, Jesus, on the cross. Jesus' blood ran across His forehead and down His sides, just like Nosy's blood on the doorposts. Benjamin put Nosy's blood there so he and his family would not die. Jesus died so that we could live with Him forever.

How can you live with Jesus forever? All you have to do is ask Jesus to forgive you for all the bad and wrong things you've done, and ask Jesus to come into your heart. When He forgives you, He will never ever remember those bad and wrong things. They are gone forever. And when He comes into your heart, the Lord and all the angels in heaven will experience elation and sing for joy and happiness.

Wouldn't you like the Lord to forgive you? Wouldn't you like Jesus to come into your heart? All you have to do is pray a prayer like this:

> Dear Lord,
>
> I'm sorry for all the bad and wrong things I've done. Please forgive me. Dear Jesus, please come into my heart. I want You and all the angels in heaven to be elated because I want to live for You.
>
> I'm sorry You had to suffer for me, but now I want to live for You and make You happy.
>
> Amen.